The Bodily Freedom Manifesto

A Speech in Three Parts

Megan Reyes

Among the many freedoms we enjoy here in the US and the freedoms due to all people of the planet, the single most important is our freedom to have control over our own bodies. Not as a country, not as a group, not even as a family, but as our own individual selves; we are owed choices for how our bodies interact with the world. For a government to deny a citizen this right is a failure of the highest order to every constituent.

Bodily autonomy, bodily integrity, bodily freedom - there are different names for this topic, but really only one meaning: a person should be free to control their body. Everyone should be free to do whatever they want to their bodies, as long as it doesn't harm anyone else, physically or mentally. You should be able to sell your own body, but you shouldn't be able to force someone else to. You should be able to do any amount of drugs you want, but you must keep in mind that your actions may affect other people's bodily freedom.

A person should be able to sell their bodies, charge however much they want, as many times as they want. A person should be able to make a decision about the future of their body without interference from others, no matter what the circumstances are or what reasons they may have. Someone getting outrageously drunk on a Saturday night can't come home to their family drunk every night, and so it should be with drugs. Have your fun, have your weekend, have your life exactly the way you want it to be, but if you let your responsibilities lapse, there will still be consequences. Alimony, child support, loss of employment, loss of social status - all of these are consequences we already live with as payment for our vices. If a person is willing to live with these negatives, that's their choice for their life.

This book isn't here to convince people to "smoke weed errday," or to go get an abortion next time the thought of being pregnant makes you sleepy, or to go see what the thousands of years of hullabaloo over prostitution is about. In fact, I want people to be able to prohibit themselves from doing things they don't agree with. Choosing not to do something is just as much an exercise in freedom as choosing to do something, and when there is a law prohibiting that something, both of these choices are taken away.

Many people may not agree with doing one or more of the things this book will discuss - that's okay. You don't have to agree on the acts to agree that true freedom allows others to perform these acts. Granting others freedom does not infringe upon your own freedom.

The point of this book is to highlight some of the things that are illegal in our lives and how arbitrary, and in most cases detrimental, these prohibitions are. These laws are not based on anything factual, they are not based on what works or doesn't work, they are not based on what's best for taxpayers. They're based on a board room meeting between a group of people you probably disagree with, making decisions about how you should live your life, formed from their personal set of morals, usually without any experience with whatever it is that they're talking about.

An argument that is often used to justify these decisions is the, "What about the children?" argument. I wholly reject this baseless argument. There are so many flaws with this argument, I hardly know where to begin.

First and foremost, I suppose, is the fact that whether or not something is illegal does not change whether it exists. Murder is illegal - it happens. Heroin is illegal - it's all over the Midwest. Having an ice cream cone in your back pocket on Sunday in Georgia is illegal - okay, that one I don't actually think happens, but is that because of the law, the disappearance of horses to lure away with said ice cream cone, or just our natural instinct to not have sticky pants? We may never know, but I am not putting an ice cream cone in my back pocket on any day, in any state, regardless of the law. Making something illegal does not make it so that it doesn't happen, and it does not make it so your children aren't exposed to it. That's the parents' job, isn't it?

I'm no expert, but I'm fairly sure that the entire populace is not responsible for what your child is exposed to. The whole idea that adults have to live in a world censored for children, is asinine. We're not children. Many of us don't have children. Why should we be creating laws for adults, designed for children? And really, that's what we're doing when we ask, "What about the children?"

The laws created to 'protect children' really just make it more difficult for adults to go about their business. The only exception seems to be homeless people sitting outside of corner stores making a good profit on simple purchases for teenagers - another example of how ineffective prohibitory laws are. At least in this hobo scenario, one that many have experienced over the years, there are some hoops for kids to jump through and, at the end of the day, the store clerk could recognize the homeless person and refuse the sale.

Is this true for pot dealers or pimps? Absolutely not. Why? Because it's illegal. There is no oversight or regulation on things that, in the eyes of the law, should not exist. The only thing the government can do is try to root out these lawbreakers - men, women, and yes, children, scattered across thousands of cities, thousands of neighborhoods, on a million different street corners, apartments, cars, offices, schools. It's basically impossible to catch them all. But do we see many instances of cigarettes or beer, or anything else for that matter, being sold in the same way? No, of course not. Sure, it exists, but on a much, much smaller scale. Why would a person risk making a sketchy transaction when they could do it from the comfort of their own business, with receipts and records and advertisement availability; with the ability to file taxes and not worry about an audit; with gaining insurance to cover their products, their families, themselves? Nobody would choose to be selling on a street corner - they do it because of the children.

"What about the children?" is an argument that halts any logical discussion about a topic and leads us down a road where our feelings and morals grip gavels and hold intellectualism hostage while we consider a populace that is already under the direct control of one or more adults. Why does the government need to control them as well? Why do others need to pay for it? (And yes, everything that is made illegal costs taxpayers money in order to enforce that status; and it still fails to completely do so.) I think it's safe to say that every parent disagrees with other parents on how to raise kids; so why do we let the government and a small group of lobbyists chime in on this? Why should the government be involved in parenting at all?

Oh, that's right, so that from a very young age we learn that it's not our parents who are in control of what we do, it's our government. We have been acquiesced to the idea that at no point in our lives are we in total control of ourselves. From birth to age 18, our rights are limited and under the control of our parental guardians. From then after, like our parents, we follow the guidelines, for our most intimate actions, set by a government most often voted in well before we are born. We don't question this, we don't think about this. All we know is our Uncle Sam's rebuke, "What about the children?"

So in response to, "What about the children?" I ask, "What about the adults?"

There are three parts to this book discussing drugs, sex, and abortion. Throughout the book, starting right now, I hope that every reader will carry this critical question with them: **If I am not allowed to control my body, who is?**

The answer is almost always multifaceted, but it always includes the government. I'm writing this book because if someone else is in control of what can, or cannot, happen to your body, You. Are. A. Slave. And I do not want to be a slave. I work for my money, I pay my taxes for my community, I vote for my rights, but I do not have to work or pay or vote to be entitled to my own damn body.

Part 1 - Drugs

In recent years, the United States has experienced an epidemic of heroin overdoses unlike anything we have seen before. In fact, last year became the worst year for overdose deaths in recent memory - as long as we ignore the deaths attributed to alcohol poisoning.

The National Institute on Alcohol Abuse and Alcoholism (NIAAA), a U.S. government entity that claims to be, "Advancing Addiction Science", has a multitude of resources and statistics on drugs, alcohol, and addiction to both. According to the NIAAA, an estimated 88,000 people die each year in the US due to alcohol.[1] That's quite a bit more than the number of heroin-related deaths in 2017, which totaled 72,306.[2] The NIAAA identifies alcohol as the third leading preventable cause of death in the US. The first two? Tobacco and poor diets, two vices also not criminally pursued by federal agencies.[1]

Further, it's not only drinkers that are affected by these alcohol-related deaths. The National Highway Traffic Safety Administration (NHTSA) reports data from 2017 showing that every day almost 30 people die in the US just from accidents involving drunk drivers. One person every 50 minutes dies, because of alcohol.[3]

Somehow though, deaths caused by illegal drugs are much more devastating than deaths caused by alcohol. Despite their best efforts, legislators have not been able to increase the penalty for death simply by outlawing the cause, so death by illegal poison is still the same as death by legal poison, and the pain it causes families is just as heart-wrenching.

So why do we allow these alcohol-related deaths to fly under the radar while fighting to end eerily similar drug-related losses? The answer is simple: because years ago our grandparents' grandparents' decided that when it came to alcohol, personal morals should not be used to pass laws.

Personal morals ushered in the 18th amendment. Nicknamed, "the noble experiment", it banned alcohol and helped cause so much crime that over the course of prohibition, homicides shot up 78%.[4] Reinforcing this, homicides drastically decreased immediately following the end of prohibition.[5]

Overall, the ban did not work. Arrests for public drunkenness and disorderly conduct only declined 50%

between 1916 and 1922, despite public drunkenness being at best essentially outlawed; at worst a worrying achievement of the mind. For the population as a whole, estimates are that consumption of alcohol declined by just 30 to 50 percent.[6] Even when made illegal, the best estimate is that only half of the population actually followed the new rule. In fact, alcohol consumption actually rose during prohibition, after taking a big hit between 1910 and 1921 due to the depression.[7]

This failure is further highlighted by the economics of prohibition. In New York, almost 75% of the state's revenue was derived from liquor taxes.[8] So when prohibition caused that revenue to be immediately lost, most states were forced to rely solely on income tax, Americans' arch-nemesis, to make up for the lost revenue. At the national level, Prohibition cost the federal government a total of $11 billion in lost tax revenue, while costing over $300 million to enforce.[8] The country deemed the "noble experiment" a morality-based failure 13 years later by passing the 21st amendment. Soon after, we were at war with the most infamous moral-based regime ever to attack freedom and the world.

Somehow, in a baffling turn of events, we once again find ourselves in the situation of morals bulldozing over personal freedoms. Less than 100 years later, we're repeating the same mistake. For 47 years the U.S. government has fought the will of the people, allowing crime to flourish while denying personal freedoms and throwing away taxpayer money, along with opportunities for tax revenue.

Today, the war on drugs, like the war on alcohol that preceded it, continues to cost Americans dearly. The war on drugs has cost over $1 trillion in the 47 years it's been active,[9] and currently costs more than $58 billion annually.[10] That's $4 billion more than the total of all proposed cuts to the 2018 U.S. budget. It's more than the total annual cost of the National Parks System and Planned Parenthood combined. Annually, the war on drugs costs Americans more than each of these government entities: the office of the president, the senate, the house, and the supreme court combined, NASA, international assistance programs, the EPA, the Department of Labor, the Department of State, the Department of Justice, the Department of the Interior, the Department of Urban Housing and Development, the Department of Homeland Security, the Department of Energy, the Department of Commerce, the corps of engineers, and the National Science Foundation.

The human cost of the war on drugs is somehow even more deplorable. 1,572, 579 people have been arrested for drug law violations. 84% of these arrests, 1,249,025 people, were arrested for possession only. For marijuana alone, 653,249 people were arrested, 89% of those, 574,641 people, were charged for possession only.[10] These are people who just want to smoke weed in their own, private lives, and we are throwing them in jail - not for free either. Our jails are

14

overflowing, and we spend $80 billion annually on corrections.[11]

Currently, legalizing marijuana use in the US is approved of by 64% of Americans.[12] Over half of our states already have some form of legalized marijuana, with recreational use being legal in 9 states. Further, despite the personal consequences, it is used daily in states where it's completely illegal. Yet everyone, regardless of how they have voted in our supposedly democratic system, is forced to pay for this war on drugs through federal taxes.

Not only does the war on drugs cost the American people billions of dollars in taxes, states that have legalized marijuana have gained billions of dollars in taxes. These funds are able to provide for social services without taxpayers having to sacrifice their paychecks. Cumulative marijuana sales in Colorado alone has reached over $4.3 billion[13] and has been recognized as contributing to an increase in tourism and jobs. In 2017, taxes gathered through marijuana sales in the state totaled over $247 million. But where does this marijuana money go exactly?

The first $40 million goes to Colorado's BEST program, which provides funds for renovating and repairing public schools that are deteriorating. This does not include the $8.4 million that goes to Colorado's Department of Education for a variety of public school needs. Another $18 million went to the Department of Public Health and Environment. From this, $7 million funded the marijuana education campaign, whose aim is to encourage young people to think about how "their goals will be easier to achieve without marijuana", while $6.7 million went to substance abuse prevention grants.[14]

Colorado is definitely the golden child of legalized marijuana, but this story is being retold in every state that has legalized its use. California estimates Prop. 64 will generate $1 billion in revenue.[15] Washington state expects to bring in $730 million over the next two years.[16] Even the slow-starting Massachusetts legalization is looking at possibly receiving $219 million in revenue over the next 2 years.[17] These tax revenues are looking increasingly appetizing to other states and yet, in the eyes of the federal government, marijuana remains illegal.

That means that the federal government can-- and does -- arrest, charge, and confiscate the goods of job makers, business owners, and tax revenue sources. All of this is done on the dime of average Americans, many of whom have clearly and loudly voted against the war on drugs.

The fact that we are paying to protect the morals of less than 36% of the country is asinine and flat out authoritarian. Worse, it seems the U.S. government has only achieved what little support it has through essentially lying about marijuana.

Although a mirror to alcohol, marijuana is instead classified as equally dangerous as heroin. Only a fool would believe that marijuana is as powerful, or as dangerous, as heroin. This classification bull-headedly ignores the fact that not only is marijuana used widely for medicinal purposes, but it can be done so safely. In fact, there have never been any reported deaths caused by the drug itself, making it safer than alcohol.

Currently, cannabis is listed as a "Schedule I substance", due to the Controlled Substances Act of 1970:

As defined by the Act, Schedule I substances are those that (1) have a high potential for abuse; (2) have no currently accepted medical use in treatment in the United States; and (3) have a lack of accepted safety for their use under medical supervision.

Literally none of these qualifications apply to marijuana; why is marijuana a Schedule I drug?

As for the first requirement, the Controlled Substances Act does not define "abuse" at all. Without this definition, abuse can be anything from smoking all day, every day, to smoking all day one time in college. Nothing is left out of laws on accident; our government is mostly composed of lawyers. Either the people who wrote the law are bad at their jobs, or they wanted ambiguity to play a role. However, using common sense, we can still take a look at abuse among marijuana users.

The NIH defines drug addiction as, "a chronic, relapsing brain disease that is characterized by compulsive drug seeking and use, despite harmful consequences." Let's assume that having an addiction is considered at least one form of abuse, and take a look at that. So, how addictive is marijuana?

The Drug Policy Alliance works towards making sure the "regulation of drugs (is) grounded in science" and has many materials discussing the effects of marijuana. According to this group, less than 10% of marijuana users meet the clinical criteria for dependence.[18] That's less than tobacco, which touts a 32% dependence rate, and less than alcohol, which causes dependence in 15% of its users.[18]

Additionally, the qualities associated with marijuana dependence are paltry. The NIH lists marijuana withdrawal symptoms on their website. "People who use marijuana frequently often report irritability, mood and sleep difficulties, decreased appetite, cravings, restlessness, and/or various forms of physical discomfort that peak within the first week after quitting and last up to 2 weeks."[19] Two whole weeks of withdrawal? That sounds terrible as long as you don't look at any information about alcohol or nicotine withdrawal!

Marijuana may have some small capacity for abuse, but it's completely misleading to say that marijuana is, "as dangerous as heroin" simply because a person might, for what will probably be less than two weeks, suffer the same symptoms as a moody teenager on a lonely Friday night.

The next requirement for Schedule I substances, is to have no currently accepted medical use in treatment in the United States. This is just patently false. The state of California legalized medical marijuana in 1996 and medical marijuana is legal today in 29 states. Doctors in these states recommend cannabis for arthritis, glaucoma, cancer, AIDS, spasticity, Parkinson's disease, and a host of other illnesses.

The fact that multiple states have doctors recommending the use of cannabis in order to fight symptoms of multiple diseases and disorders means that the third requirement for a Schedule I substance doesn't apply to marijuana either. Having medical professionals in over half of our states endorse its use clearly establishes that it does not, "have a lack of accepted safety for their use under medical supervision".

Funnily enough, all of these requirements are met by two familiar substances that are perfectly legal and easy to get a hold of: nicotine and alcohol. While some fringe opinions suggest nicotine for help with concentration and Parkinson's disease, smoking cigarettes or taking nicotine in any form, is not something that is recommended on a regular basis, in any state. Drinking alcohol certainly is not used for anything medical, with the exception of alcohol withdrawal, and only then in severe cases.

So actually, it's really not that funny at all. Our government prevents us from enjoying marijuana while allowing people as young as 18 to partake in cigarettes and then later alcohol, both of which fit the description of, "as bad as heroin" better than the devil's lettuce. If the government believes that a person should be free to decide to use nicotine or alcohol products, it should believe that a person should be free to use a much less harmful drug.

But then, it isn't all about health to the government. They also care about our quality of life, which is why the law punishes us most severely when we threaten our own happiness through "bad decisions". Federal laws regarding marijuana often have "mandatory sentencing", which means that even if the judge wanted to, they would have no power to give less than the mandatory sentence.

While possession is only a misdemeanor for the first two offenses, three or more possession offenses is a felony. Any other activity, including sale or cultivation, involving marijuana is also a felony. Being marked as a felon will ruin a person's life - forever. Being named a felon should be a moniker for dangerous individuals, but the fact of the matter is, a felon could simply be a person who happened to get caught with a joint three times.

The argument can be made that such unlucky people simply should've followed the law, but why is this even the law? Why is the law designed to be more devastating than the act it's trying to prevent? Why is it that the worst punishment, the worst possible scenario of smoking marijuana is that the federal government catches you?

The entire war on drugs is not an exercise in the U.S. government protecting its citizens, but rather a moral stance led by a minority of our representatives. Even drugs that that have the scariest reputations would serve the public best by being made readily available for purchase. Heroin is one such drug.

The classification that makes heroin highly illegal only makes it so that heroin is more dangerous to the public. The average unprofessional drug dealer has little to no quality control, and often even less of an idea of what they're doing when they make heroin. This lack of oversight and regulation holds up the argument that drugs acquired on the streets are inherently more dangerous than those acquired through legal channels. This is especially apparent when we look at one of the main causes of heroin addiction: legal opioids.

The NIH reports on their website that 80% of people using heroin took prescription drugs before starting heroin. Another 75% said that the first opioid they had was a prescription drug.[20] Fentanyl, one of these prescription drugs, has been accused of being a large part of why heroin overdoses have been on the rise. This is only somewhat true.

Fentanyl is usually mixed with heroin when produced by illegal entities, as it is known to raise the potency of heroin. This causes overdoses because most people who receive heroin mixed with fentanyl do not know it. If some kind of control was available, maybe something like...the regulations that already exist to make fentanyl safe to use, heroin overdoses would most likely see a drastic decline.

What exactly is fentanyl? It's a drug commonly prescribed to patients for dealing with the effects of cancer or to reduce pain after surgery. Beyond the drug being described as very easy to overdose and very difficult to self-gauge dosages, it is very much like heroin. In fact, the main two differences between heroin and fentanyl are: (1)fentanyl is 50 times more potent than heroin and, (2)fentanyl is legal.[21]

How could this be? How could such a powerful drug be given out to people? First and foremost, fentanyl is not dangerous when used properly, when used with a doctor's supervision. Fentanyl helps many people in pain and is an important drug for those who need it. Secondly, fentanyl is not the strongest drug we give to people. Morphine is 100 times more potent than heroin; hydrocodone is just as strong as morphine. Oxycodone is 50% stronger than morphine, while methadone is three times as strong as morphine.[21] All of these drugs are listed as Schedule II, meaning that while they have a potential for abuse, they also have medically accepted uses and are therefore available to large swaths of the population.

So while we know for sure that drugs very similar to, and even stronger than, heroin are safe when used properly and made in a controlled setting, we outlaw heroin. We are told how dangerous heroin is over and over again, and then we take steps to ensure that it is truly as dangerous as possible. The illegality of heroin guarantees that there is no regulation, no oversight, and no control over what is actually being bought and sold. After all, you don't need to guarantee quality for something that has been made illegal; it shouldn't exist anymore.

The argument may be made that creating a system where someone can more easily become addicted to heroin is a bad thing. Definitely; I think we can all agree that addiction is bad. However, based on information gathered by the U.S. government itself, approximately 80% of heroin users, who comprise only 0.2% of all U.S. adults, never actually become addicted to their drug.[20] Meanwhile, 12.7% of all U.S. adults are currently addicted to alcohol.[22] But that's okay; that's normal.

If and when a person decides to get clean there are many ways to do so. In the U.S. most patients are treated at methadone clinics, where methadone is given in a supervised environment and drug tests are administered frequently. Although methadone is essentially the same thing as heroin, it has a "dampened" high, making it 'okay' to sell, despite actually being more powerful than heroin.

Another common solution is buprenorphine, usually prescribed as either "Suboxone" or "Subutex", and is similar to methadone and heroin in effects. There are two bonuses to buprenorphine, however: it does not have a "dampened" high, and you can take it home. Again, this is totally fine. Is it pretty much take-out heroin? Yes. But is it dangerous? Not according to the government, so it's fine! Why is it fine, according to the government? Because a doctor is providing the medicine from a controlled and regulated source, while simultaneously educating their patient on dosage and risks with other substances. This is impossible to do with heroin - because it's illegal.

Another common treatment, though not endorsed by the FDA, is marijuana. Studies have shown that cannabis, despite what the U.S. government claims, is not only more effective at treating pain than opioids, but also can help with recovering from addiction to these drugs. In a 2012 paper, published in Journal of Psychoactive Drugs, studies showed that marijuana prevents building a tolerance to opioids and can actually help 'reset' tolerance for current opioid users. The study also suggested that cannabinoids may reduce not only cravings for opiates, but may reduce the severity of withdrawal as well.[23]

The idea of drugs being illegal simply hurts those who are in need most. In the U.K., actual heroin is used to help addicts, with good results so far. Across the pond, addicts can legally be "weaned off" the drug and, eventually, get their lives back.

Heroin prescriptions have been a part of the UK since the 1920's and have helped many people get off the drug completely. One such system, the Randomised Injecting Opioid Treatment Trial, RIOTT, started in 2005 and since then, Britain's heroin addicts have had profound changes in their lives. This program originally involved 127 heroin addicts who had failed to kick the habit through more traditional treatments. After treatment, more than half of participants were said to be "largely abstinent", while 1 in 5 did not use street heroin at all. About 75% of the addicts said that the prescriptions "substantially" reduced their drug use.[24]

Heroin addicts, as many are quick to forget, are not only trapped by their chemical addiction, but also by the monetary repercussions that come along with drug abuse. This often makes it impossible for drug users to leave their toxic environments, even once they have a moment of clarity and want to get out. Through RIOTT, not only were these people able to start the path to recovery, but they were given the opportunity to spend about $70 per week on legal heroin. This replaced the $425 they had been spending every week, just to support their habit.[24]

We have multiple answers to our heroin problem; we can help those addicted through proven methods and yet, instead of implementing these solutions, we spend billions tightening regulations and turning victims into criminals. We do this not only in the name of higher morals, but also in the name of false information about drug abuse, addiction, and drug availability.

While the U.K. treatment programs cost more than traditional chemical ones, they are so much more effective, and help prevent the spread of diseases like HIV. In fact, legalizing heroin would allow for more education on proper use of the drug such as using clean needles, checking dosages, dangerous drug mixes, and many other simple facts that could save lives. In any case, these programs are much more cost effective.

Jail time costs anywhere from $25k to $59k per person, per year, depending on what state you look at. RIOTT's heroin program cost just over $21k per person, per year, and at the end a person's life had been completely turned around for the better.

Legalizing drugs would not just help drug users, it would also help solve problems that plague a number of states: drug cartels. The Guardian reported in early 2018 that, "when a state on the Mexican border legalised medical use of the drug, violent crime fell by 13% on average...Homicides specifically related to the drug trade fell by an astonishing 41%." The article goes on to suggest that cartels are moving away from marijuana and into producing their own heroin, in order to avoid legal competition.[25]

With regulation, drugs can be created and sold safely. With legalization, crime related to drugs would decline, users could be educated in the proper use and dosage of a drug, kids would have more hoops to jump through and thus have less access to drugs, and tax revenue could improve communities. The government getting involved in regulating whether or not we should be allowed to use drugs has done nothing but cost Americans money, increase crime, and fill our prisons. The logic behind these laws is fundamentally flawed at best, intentionally oppressive at worst.

To be told what you may or may not do to your own body is an assault on freedom for every person forced under these laws. You don't have to agree with doing drugs to agree that democracy should reign over the personal opinions of our legislature. Again and again states vote for this right, and again and again the outcomes of these votes are postponed or vetoed in their own states, and then fully dismissed as invalid in the eyes of the federal government. Having less control over your own body than your government is tantamount to slavery, and yet continues to be a pervasive force in our modern government.

Part 2 - Sex

Prostitute.

The word itself is nearly taboo and jabs like an expletive. Yet for many of us, only one thing separates us from being considered prostitutes: we don't get paid when we have sex.

Anecdotal evidence of the stigma surrounding prostitution, and the harm it causes, is constantly provided to nearly every country in the world. In fact, International Day to End Violence Against Sex Workers began as a memorial for the deaths of at least 71 women at the hands of the Green River killer in Seattle, Washington. Most of the 71 women were prostitutes, who make for easy targets because they are overlooked and often blamed for any violence against them; after all, that's what they get for being prostitutes, right?

The way that we talk about prostitutes, starting with the fact that 'prostitute' is such a stigmatized word that it isn't typically used when advocating for their rights, is designed to dehumanize them. They are not given an opportunity to voice their thoughts and when they try to anyway, they are told that they are victims and that they do not know or understand what they are doing. Even those that 'support' prostitutes and their rights claim that anti-prostitution laws 'help women', but that is emphatically not true. In fact, these laws simply take autonomy away from consenting adults.

Though rife with a history of slavery and kidnapping, modern prostitution can provide a safe and steady income with flexible schedules helpful to parents and students - when it's legal. Unfortunately, under the current laws in various countries across the globe, including our own, there are two very different sides to prostitution, two very different images we often see when talking about prostitution.

In one, we can only see suffering - children and adults, stolen and sold, forced to be raped by strangers until they die or miraculously escape; women trying to earn fast money, only to be sucked into drug abuse and conned out of their earnings; women being put in jail by police claiming to 'help' them; business owners or criminals reaping the benefits of these tricks and horrors, making more money than most college graduates, and not paying a dime in taxes all the while.

In the other, we see choice and confidence - safety and good health; benefits and a w-2; labor laws that actually protect prostitutes; money being put directly into the hands of prostitutes - giving women, transgenders, and men another opportunity to both work and have time to study, spend time with family, travel - whatever they want to do. It gives them freedom.

Most anti-prostitution advocates fight against this freedom by claiming that prostitutes have a "false consciousness" and don't understand what they are doing. These advocates strip prostitutes of their autonomy and humanity before proceeding with their arguments, a tactic most governments don't seem to mind. Regardless, Amnesty International warns, "It is necessary to avoid the stereotyping of all sex workers as lacking in agency or capacity as this is harmful and disempowering, and not reflective of evidence regarding the situations and experiences of sex workers globally."[29]

Diminishing the lives of all prostitutes to a single profile of a woman in need of rescue is not a new strategy to deny women enterprising opportunities. However, in the case of prostitution it's not only women's rights that are being subverted. Sex-Law expert Belinda Brooks-Gordon argues that claiming that anti-prostitution laws are beneficial to women, "completely undermines the argument or the evidence that 25% of men who pay for sex pay other men for sex."[26] Additionally, in 2014, The Telegraph reported that 42% of prostitutes in the UK were male.[27] As for the rest of the world, a study released in 2018 showed that at least 20% of prostitutes worldwide are male.[28] Prostitution is not a women's rights issue; it's a human rights issue.

Although the face of human trafficking is often sex-related, the reality is that only 19% of trafficked people are sex workers,[69] and so prostitution laws have a difficult time curtailing human trafficking on the whole. When looking at human trafficking numbers, the number of cases does increase in countries where legalized prostitution is found - more than likely meaning that these traffickers are being reported and caught. While another possible explanation is that legal prostitution causes increased human trafficking, there is not enough evidence to support this. In fact, there is equal evidence that supports the idea that illegal prostitution causes increased human trafficking. A study done in 2011 suggested a third explanation, "...prostitution laws have no effect on whether there is any reported incidence of trafficking..."[68] The data from that study also suggested that cracking down on prostitution is, "likely to increase rather than decrease trafficking flows."[68] Further, a report by The London School of Economics and Political Science found that, "the legalization of prostitution is not equal to laxer enforcement of anti-trafficking laws and, conversely, the fact that prostitution is illegal does not imply stricter anti-trafficking enforcement. Human trafficking always remains illegal even if prostitution becomes legal."[70] There is still very little data on human trafficking; we only have rough estimates of trafficking numbers and it is assumed that most trafficked people are never found. Yet, it is known that most trafficking rings operate successfully because they can hide in the shadows of our society, shadows that we have the full power to shed light on.

Many of the issues associated with illegal prostitution are actually issues with women's rights. Anti-prostitution groups fight against prostitution in order to prevent things like rape, slavery, assault, and underpayment. All of these things are already illegal. None of these things are found, without serious legal consequences, in any legitimate business. Why is it assumed that the government could ignore these laws in the case of a legal brothel? In a legitimate business, steps can be taken to make sure that the women are safe, that they are healthy, and that every part of their prostitution is their choice.

Conversely, while illegal prostitution's impact on human trafficking may need more research and discussion, there is little room for debate on what kind of impact anti-prostitution laws have on prostitutes currently in the U.S. and many other developed countries. Multiple studies have found that illegal prostitution directly causes more dangerous situations for prostitutes. A San Francisco study found that, "82% had been assaulted and 68% had been raped while working as prostitutes."[33] In another study, done in Colorado, prostitutes were found to be, "18 times more likely to be murdered than non-prostitutes their age and race."[33] One of the driving forces behind these statistics are prostitutes' lack of labor rights and their inability to go to the police without being prosecuted.

Prostitutes in the U.K. often avoid contacting police because it usually causes them to be evicted or otherwise harassed. This has caused "pop-up brothels" where prostitutes can feel safe to carry out their business. A London prostitute told The Guardian in 2017 that her place had CCTV and a panic button, and that she, "can't imagine working any other way now".[39] Despite the safety that prostitutes may enjoy in these settings, police continue to crack down on prostitutes. They do this despite the National Police Chiefs' Council having acknowledged, "simple enforcement does not produce sustainable outcomes and can actually increase the vulnerability of sex workers to violent attack."[39]

Similarly, a prostitute in Oslo, Norway, told Amnesty International that she was "essentially punished" by police after reporting a rape at knife point. "[W]e went back to the house and, two days later, the landlord threw us out. The police put pressure on the landlord. She gave us half a day to get out."[40] The 2016 article by The Nation stated that in Oslo,

35

"Sex workers reported routine harassment by police, targeting migrant and Nigerian sex workers in particular." Amnesty International corroborated this information by saying that Norwegian police "used sex workers' reports of violence to facilitate their eviction and/or their deportation."[40]

The deterrent of being labeled a criminal also affects the spread of STDs. Many reports, including a 2012 New York City study conducted by the Urban Justice Center, show a history of police using condoms as evidence against prostitutes. The fear of generating evidence that could be used against them often causes prostitutes to simply forgo condom use altogether.[34] Rolling Stone reported in 2016 that decriminalization would reduce, "HIV epidemics across all settings, averting 33-46 percent of HIV infections in the next decade. Such a move would also reduce mistreatment of sex workers and increase their access to human rights, including health care."[35]

Many states, and many countries, in an attempt to 'compromise' have adopted laws meant to reduce prostitution using what is called, "the Nordic model". The laws of the Nordic Model are written so the clients are the ones who are criminalized instead of the prostitutes. The thought behind this is that prostitutes will feel safe to come to police with assault and robbery cases - but this just isn't what happens.

What happens is that prostitutes suffer. According to Amnesty International, laws criminalizing prostitution consumers, "regularly force sex workers to operate covertly and/or prohibit actions that sex workers take to manage their safety and, in doing so, violate sex workers' human rights," and, "also creates an environment where law enforcement officers and other officials can perpetrate violence, harassment and extortion against sex workers with impunity."[37]

Ann Jordan, of the Center for Human Rights & Humanitarian Law, reported, "The experiment has failed. In the 13 years since the law was enacted, the Swedish government has been unable to prove that the law has reduced the number of sex buyers or sellers or stopped trafficking."[41]

The United Nations Programme on HIV/AIDS, has said, "The approach of criminalising the client has been shown to backfire on sex workers." Clarifying, "There is very little evidence to suggest that any criminal laws related to sex work stop demand for sex or reduce the number of sex workers. Rather, all of them create an environment of fear and marginalisation for sex workers, who often have to work in remote and unsafe locations to avoid arrest of themselves or their clients."[42]

Meanwhile, in countries and states that have decriminalized or fully legalized prostitution, the women not only feel safer, but actually are safer. A study done by the Christchurch School of Medicine found that 90% of prostitutes in New Zealand, "believed the PRA [Prostitution Reform Act] gave them employment, legal and health and safety rights. A substantial 64 percent found it easier to refuse clients."[30] Research done by the University of Nevada found that 84% of prostitutes there felt that their job was, "safe."[31] Photographer Marc McAndrews spent five years documenting brothels in Nevada, providing Business Insider with images of clean and organized houses, hotels, and rooms;[32] a stark contrast with the streets and woods prostitutes are often forced to use when their work is illegal.

In Switzerland, prostitution has been legal for 76 years. In response to complaints about noise and traffic jams, the city of Zurich voted five years ago to build "sex boxes", drive-in structures that resemble car garages where prostitutes and their customers can meet. These boxes accommodate not only cars, but motorcycles as well. These boxes are just another step towards ensuring that prostitution is treated like any other service industry. Some even have beds, and all of them come with an alarm button that will alert security, although no serious incidents have happened so far. After five years, city spokeswoman Nadeen Schuster said that they had achieved the goal to, "improve the working conditions of sex workers – their health, physical and mental integrity."[45]

In 2014, the Washington Post reported about when Rhode Island accidentally legalized prostitution. A 2003 court case brought to light the fact that the state of Rhode Island, while able to prosecute crimes such as streetwalking, pimping, and trafficking, could not legally prevent prostitution. This error, made in 1980, was not an issue until the internet arrived, providing opportunities for prostitutes to advertise their services without streetwalking. From 2003 until legislators revised the law in 2009, gonorrhea among women declined by 39%, while reported rape declined by 31%.[46]

Decriminalization of prostitution creates safer, healthier environments for prostitutes, but even when prostitution is made legal, restrictions and a lack of regulation can still lead to situations that cause women's rights, and the rights of others, to be skirted. Nevada is certainly a step in the right direction with requirements for health records, weekly STD testing, and partnerships between brothels and local police. Prostitutes' lives in Nevada have been improved, but there is still much to be done regarding their autonomy. The primary problem is the fact that currently the law states that only licensed businesses may sell sex. This basically recreates, and sanctifies, a system where workers often must rely on a 'pimp' and can easily be exploited.

According to The Nevada Independent, some brothels keep as much as half of a woman's earnings and force the woman to pay for her own state-required STD tests (without which she cannot work), her licensing fee (which again, cannot be used anywhere else but licensed brothels), her own taxes, rent, food, and other expenses associated with her job.[36]

Recently the state tried to require that five dollars per day be paid in taxes by the customer. As reported in the same Nevada Independent article, published in 2018, most prostitutes do not charge less than $1,000. That means in many cases, a customer would have been paying less than 0.5% in taxes for sexual services. Luckily, this did not pass.

Unluckily, the reason this tax did not get approved was because our legislature elected to not tax prostitution in Nevada at all. Republican Gov. Jim Gibbons explains, "I'm not a supporter of legalizing prostitution in Nevada. So by taxing it, there's a recognition of the legality of it. And that's all I want to say."[36] Prostitution is one of the only topics on which our representatives will proudly proclaim that they will not acknowledge what people have voted for and what is legal, but instead will only acknowledge things that they believe should be legal, regardless of what our 'democratic system' has decided.

Brothels in Nevada are subject to federal income tax and local fees, but otherwise are exempt from entertainment tax and have no other state taxes attached to them. So not only are brothel owners taking an obscene cut from their workers, but they aren't even paying taxes to the communities they operate in. All because of some moral high ground taken on by representatives that flaunt their refusal to represent the will of their constituents.

These kinds of policies highlight the fact that no one in power cares about the people in this industry, the communities surrounding these industries, or even their sworn duty to represent their state. This dismissive attitude is not new and not surprising.

According to current laws, the women and men that make up the industry of prostitution do not matter. The laws created to prevent prostitution and brothels are so blatantly moral-based and devoid of any supporting evidence, that even fake prostitutes are seen as a threat to our government.

In September of 2018, a Canadian-based company attempted to set up a "try-before-you-buy" sex doll shop in Houston, Texas. The shop met strong opposition from the city council and a Christian group that claims to be against all forms of pornography. By October, the city council had succeeded in completely preventing the shop from opening. How did they manage this? They simply modified an existing city ordinance to prevent this business, and any others like it, from opening.

While Mayor Sylvester Turner said he didn't want to be "the moral police", that's exactly what he became. His reasoning? "We do need to be very mindful of what comes into our city and what our children and others may be exposed to."[43] And others, meaning the consenting, voting

41

adults whose actions and opinions the city has completely circumvented.

Laws are meant to protect and help people, and usually a victim must be present in order to argue that a law fulfills this duty. Who is the victim in a shop of sex dolls? Brooks-Gordon has spoken on this idea as well, "There is no reason to criminalise prostitution clients when you cannot show demonstrable harm. In fact all the evidence is in the other direction, that it is harmful to criminalise."[26] She went on to say that criminalizing can lead to blackmail, such as councilman Greg Travis threatened to do in Houston.

Greg Travis, a member of the city council of Houston, "said he planned to record the business' patrons entering the building and shame them online," according to USA Today. He went on to say, "This is not a good business for our city. We are not Sin City."[44] With no discussion and no vote, sixteen people decided to change the law for 2.3 million people, to clarify that having sex with a robot was 'a sin.' There isn't any empirical evidence as of yet, but it's safe to assume neither the bible nor God has given a ruling on sex robots. Even if some brave scholar went through the bible and did find the line in Revelations about sex-technology advancements, that would not justify this moral stance being forced upon constituents who may or may not agree with Christian ideals.

But again, non-Christian ideals don't matter; men don't matter; women don't matter - none of the people that are actually affected by legislation on prostitution matter. If they did matter, prostitution would be legalized because in the places where it is, the benefits are empirical.

Many "examples" of prostitution causing more abuse, rape, or trafficking are based on misleading studies and muddied statistics. Every case regarding prostitution and increased rape, mistreatment, or low wages, are cases that do not have fully legalized prostitution. These cases, such as in Nevada's situation, do not give rights to prostitutes to sell their body, but instead give rights to the buildings which house the services. If a person was free to simply apply for a license and get regular health checks before offering sexual services, that person could become an entrepreneur. Instead they are forced to rely on what are essentially pimps disguised as brothel owners in order to legally fund their chosen profession, once again taking the power away from the individual prostitutes - the ones that are actually working - and giving it to an overseer.

There is absolutely no reason why a person should not be free to sell their body. With regulations such as inspections, health code standards, licensing, and labor laws, prostitution can operate very similarly to how other parts of the sex industry are currently controlled. When it comes to consenting adults, there is little room or need for government in sexual affairs.

The strongest arguments against prostitution are based on morals that not everyone shares. They are not based in fact, and often are based in debunked statistics and stereotypes. Arguments in favor of prostitution are scientifically based and have clear, contemporary examples throughout the globe.

The United States in particular has an obligation to its' people to uphold democracy over personal morals. Perhaps the argument can be made that morals are more important than democracy, but it cannot be claimed that personal morals may stampede over the votes of the public and that our government is a democratic one. You don't have to ever be willing to sell your body, but telling someone else that they may not sell their body takes away their freedom to choose how to live their life.

Part 3 - Abortion

In the U.S. we have the right to an abortion. However, that right is consistently under pressure, debate, and, in some states, wrapped in an intolerable amount of red tape. Roe v Wade ushered in an open debate about abortion rights in the U.S., but overall insured hardly any rights, including those typically associated with the case.

While Roe v Wade specifically says that a woman's right to privacy includes her right to an abortion, it goes on to say that it is a state's responsibility to protect a woman's health and the potential for life. States are legally allowed to pass legislation that affect a fetus once it reaches "viability", or the ability to live outside of the womb. However, there are currently no federal laws that define this "viability" or the responsibility of the mother once this stage is reached. Most states have chosen to read this "viability" as the point where a mother cannot abort the fetus.

This is just ridiculous. If the fetus is able to live outside of the womb, why is the pregnant woman still responsible for it? And if it cannot live outside of the womb, well then it hasn't reached "viability" yet, has it? Either way, the woman should be protected by Roe v Wade and have access to an abortion at any point, but this simply isn't how legislators in many states have decided to interpret the ruling.

This clinging to Christian ideals about abortion and the evolutionary job of women as breeding bitches to be used as baby dispensaries, is the entire source of the arguments surrounding abortion in the U.S. Women are talked about and treated as animals, despite the fact that this issue has been taken to court time and time again and found to be an issue over which politicians should have no control. Women who want an abortion are accused of "not knowing what's best for them" and "ignorant of their evil." They are almost never accused of being their own person, of having a right to their bodies, of making the right choice for themselves.

Women are in charge of their own bodies. This is either true, or not true. You cannot cherry pick when it is true and when it is not. Well, legally you can, because multiple states have done it and continue to do it.

The number one goal, and outcome, of anti-abortion laws is the assertion that women should not be allowed to decide what grows inside of their bodies. In theory, the ruling on Planned Parenthood of Southeastern Pennsylvania v Casey prevents states from placing substantial obstacles or undue burdens on women seeking abortions; in reality it has made it very difficult to fight anything related to abortion restrictions short of outright bans.

This is why nine states have as few as two abortion clinics for the entire state, while five more have just one.[47] Two of these states, Delaware and Rhode Island, could argue that they're so geographically small that they really only need the three clinics that they have. The other twelve states can make no such argument. In West Virginia, only two clinics are available for nearly 400,000 women of childbearing age, while South Carolina's three clinics are supposed to be able to serve over 1 million women of childbearing age. The populations of Idaho, Utah, Nebraska, Oklahoma, and Arkansas are much smaller than other states, at least according to popular opinions such as the moniker "fly-over state" suggests. So perhaps the argument that three clinics is sufficient could be made based on population levels and the omission of the fact that, with the exception of Nebraska, most women in these states do not live in a county with a clinic.[71]

The five states with one clinic though? Wyoming, North Dakota, South Dakota, Mississippi, and Missouri - touting approximately 10 times the population of the former three states listed and 2 times the population of Mississippi - have somehow skirted abortion rights. Mississippi in particular, one of our favorite "worst of all" states, has essentially denied women access to abortion clinics without any obstacles.

What part of one clinic for over 1 million women is not a substantial obstacle or an undue burden? Is it the part where a woman must make no less than two trips to the clinic because the law says that she must have a 'counsel' session - counseling clearly designed to dissuade her from abortion with pamphlets that read, "Life begins at conception", despite no supporting scientific evidence to back this - and then return no less than 72 hours later? Or is the undue burden avoided earlier than that, when she must pay separately for abortion coverage from her private health insurance provider because state law says that health insurance companies cannot include abortion coverage as part of a health insurance package? Or perhaps having the one clinic in Mississippi be unable to perform abortions after 16 weeks - due to extra regulations, despite the law stating that 20 weeks is the cut off - is not considered a substantial obstacle?[48]

But once again, it doesn't matter. Women don't matter, voters don't matter - the law doesn't matter. Because once again, our representatives think that their personal morals are more important than laws and Supreme Court decisions.

Many of our representatives have openly stated that they think Roe v Wade was a mistake and that they would like to see it undone. While this is more than likely a line to ensure certain votes and not an actual plan, it's still very easy, too easy, for abortion rights to be blocked and made more difficult to access, as is evident in Mississippi's case.

Anti-abortion activists say they are in favor of protecting life, both of the 'child' and of the mother, but this simply isn't true. Abortion was outlawed once before, and we know the outcome. In 1965, 17% of deaths related to pregnancy were due to illegal abortions.[49] The ban didn't work, and directly led to the deaths of women. Yet 'pro-life' groups fight to return to these times, despite the fact that legal abortions have only a 0.3% chance of death when performed at any point during the pregnancy and only a 0.05% chance of death if performed during the first trimester.[49]

Sadly, this argument of 'protecting women and children' is typical. Abortion is currently treated with as little regard to empirical evidence as possible, despite a wealth of both social and scientific data in place as part of our medical laws. First, women in 14 states are forced to undergo an ultrasound,[50] a medical procedure not required for a first-trimester abortion except under these state laws.[51] Regardless of whether there is a medical reason for these ultrasounds, they are still performed simply to try and guilt the patient into not going through with the abortion.

In 28 states women are also required to listen to 'abortion counseling' information, which is often not only skewed, but forces the woman to wait a period of time between hearing the information and actually having the abortion. In fact, many states have mandates requiring that specific materials be read to a woman before an abortion. This idea may sound like a good one, except for the fact that many parts of these materials, in many states, are complete fiction.[50]

In 7 of the aforementioned 28 states, the required information asserts that there is a link between abortion and breast cancer.[50] There is no link between abortion and breast cancer. This idea has been debunked by the National Cancer Institute, the American Cancer Society, and the American College of Obstetricians and Gynecologists.[50]

In four states, a link is implied between abortion and possible infertility,[50] a claim that has been debunked for decades. Also in four states, is the false idea that abortion patients suffer from a form of PTSD after the procedure. Referred to as "post abortion syndrome", this effect is simply not real. Both the American Psychological Association (APA) and the American Psychiatric Association refuse to support such a claim. The APA has gone as far as to state flatly, "there is no credible evidence that a single elective abortion of an unwanted pregnancy in and of itself causes mental health problems for adult women".[52]

Meanwhile, actual pregnancy does have a psychological illness after-effect: postpartum depression. According to the National Institute on Mental Health, 15% of new mothers have postpartum depression,[53] while a study done in 2010 found that around 10% of new fathers also suffered this form of depression.[54] This illness is caused by the sudden drop in hormones after giving birth, often exacerbated by sleep deprivation due to a new baby being in the house.

Real health issues aside, after reading and listening to lies and half-truths, women seeking an abortion are not through the gauntlet yet. Next, each state's mandated materials have a section with visual representations of fetuses. Only 42% of these images are described as "completely accurate."[50] Most of the inaccuracies are meant to make fetuses look more like babies, because who could look at a baby and not want one?

A lot of women, actually. According to a 2016 study conducted by the National Survey of Family Growth, only half of women were expecting to have children in the future. Of women who had not yet had children, 20% said they did not want children in the future. Among first-time mothers, that number jumped up to 50%.[55]

While many arguments against abortion cite medical issues, the fact of the matter is that pregnancy is one of the most taxing medical events a person can possibly go through.

53

Not allowing a woman to have access to an abortion means that some women are forced to go through pregnancy. This includes nine months of nausea, bloating, bleeding gums, hemorrhoids, swelling, nosebleeds, yeast infections, pain, stretch marks, insomnia, changes in appetite, and in some cases gestational diabetes, which even after birth causes half of afflicted women to develop type 2 diabetes.[56]

These side effects say nothing about the cost, physical and financial, of giving birth, either. An hours long delivery, pain, missed work, and worst of all for women in need, medical bills. According to the Economist, the average U.S. birth costs more than the most recent royal birth in the U.K.[57] We are currently the most expensive nation to give birth in, with average estimates ranging from $10,808 to $51,125, according to the Guardian.[58] One woman, Apo Osae-Twum, gave birth to premature triplets and was billed an agonizing $877,000. Though insurance may cover much of these costs, without the Affordable Care Act many people wouldn't have affordable insurance; even with this act in place, many people still do not have insurance.

Even with the help of insurance, the high cost of giving birth does not even include trips to the doctors, prenatal medicine, or all of the safety features new parents must install into their homes and cars when they bring home a child. Even with the help of insurance, Mrs. Osae-Twum and her family ended up owing $51,000.[58]

Not all women needing financial aid want to have an abortion or give up their baby. One way expecting mothers who would like to keep their child, but may not be able to afford to do so, can avoid having an abortion to prevent destitution is to rely on Planned Parenthood. Currently however, Planned Parenthood is under fire and in danger of being wildly defunded by the same legislators claiming to be defending mothers-to-be and their incoming babies. Many anti-abortion advocates are in favor of this, claiming that, despite federal spending reports showing otherwise, Planned Parenthood does not provide enough healthcare to expecting mothers in comparison with their abortion services.

While the entire country seems to get up-in-arms about Planned Parenthood using just 3% of its funds to perform abortions, these heated arguments do not surround the same taxpayer money going towards anti-abortion efforts. In 2016, the state of Ohio spent $1million on pro-life clinics,[59] places that are unregulated and often delay, mislead, and pressure women into choosing to have a child rather than get an abortion. Most states also have license plates that are pro-life and fund pro-life clinics. Only two states have pro-choice license plates: California and Virginia.

So while anti-abortion groups lament having their tax money pay for abortions, pro-choice groups are expected to sit quietly while their tax money goes to religion-based clinics that spread misinformation unchecked?

The information I gathered about both Planned Parenthood and these pro-life clinics have made me unsure the government should be funding any specific clinics related to pregnancy (and to be sure, a whole other book could be written on this subject). Rather, government funding should be available to be given directly to women, not organizations with certain 'best interests' in mind, so each individual woman may have the power to choose for themselves how and where to care for their bodies. Women should be entitled to receive aid from the government in pregnancy matters without legislators being entitled to interfere with a woman's choice of health insurance, clinic, doctor, or procedure.

While legislators claim that these anti-abortion regulations are all in the best interest of children, other policies tell a different story. About half of the states in the US currently have no minimum age for marriage,[60] and children are allowed to be married if their parents think it is in their best interest. States such as Florida, Maine, Louisiana, Kentucky, New Mexico, and New Jersey have no age limit on marriage, while others practice some control; Massachusetts waits until girls are 13 before approving marriage. Once married, many states allow what would be statutory rape, if not for the marriage certificate.[60]

So not only is the government taking away women's right to have an abortion by limiting access to abortion clinics, they also continue to allow parents to strip away the right to choose when to have a partner in marriage and when to have sex with said partner. Most of these child marriages are forced onto girls that have gotten pregnant - often through rape - who are told that the only way to make it 'right' is to marry whoever impregnated them.

According to Frontline, between 2000 and 2015, 207,459 minors were married in the U.S.; 87% of those minors were girls. 985 of these children were 14 years old, 51 of them were 13, and 6 were 12 years old.[61] These are small percentages but, this shouldn't be happening at all in the United States. We're supposed to be upholding freedom and allowing children to grow up in safe environments. These policies do not allow this to happen. What possible reason could there be for marrying a 12 year old? Could it be that they married another 12 year old?

Unlikely, since 86% of these minors married adults. In fact, 31 adults that married a child were over 60 years old; 61 adults were in their 50's, and 368 adults were in their 40's.[61] Author of American Child Bride: A History of Minors and Marriage in the United States told Frontline, "Almost all the evidence indicates that girls in cities don't get married young, that girls from middle class or wealthy families, don't get married young...This is a rural phenomenon and it is a phenomenon of poverty."

While our current regulations and laws surrounding abortion may not have been designed to harm those living in poverty worst of all, that has been the outcome. These children have been left behind, and when they get pregnant they will be trapped in a marriage and family that has completely betrayed them and their best interests. They may look to their government for help, but if they live in a state where their representative has taken a stance against abortion instead of child marriage, they will receive no such aid. In many states, just to get an abortion, minors must have the signatures of their parents. In many states, a married woman must have the signature of her husband.

A pregnant child bride will more than likely be forced to give birth under these circumstances. The only people able to help her out of an unwanted pregnancy are the ones who caused the pregnancy in the first place, against the child's will, and her government, which has said that she does not know more about what she wants than her parents or husband.

The entire system surrounding abortion has cultivated an environment that prevents women from having control over their bodies and choices. Similar to Jim Crow laws, the only exception to this stripping away of rights is the fact that abortion is technically legal under federal law. In every other aspect, it seems, legislators do their best to skirt the legalization in order to force their own morals upon the will of the people. Not only do these actions make Roe v Wade nearly impossible to honor, but they also bring down the women, and men, involved.

This problem disproportionally affects low-income women. It is known that low income levels, low education, and race negatively contributes to high teen birth. Girls in foster care are more than twice as likely to become pregnant as girls that are not in foster care. While the pregnancy rate for black teens and hispanic teens are 93 and 74 per 1,000, respectively, the rate for non-hispanic white teens is just 35 per 1,000. According to the CDC, rural communities had nearly ⅓ more teen pregnancies than urban areas.[62]

A young couple with bright futures can see all of their hard work and dreams shattered because of a very fixable mistake. Only 38% of girls who give birth before age 18 receive their high school diplomas by age 22, compared to 90% of girls that do not get pregnant during adolescence.[62] Further, the CDC and the Department of Human Health and Services (HHS) outline a recurring system of poverty and teen pregnancy.

HHS reports that compared to non-childbearing teens, teen mothers are more likely to rely on public assistance,[63] and the CDC reports that low education levels and low income of their family is a cause of teen pregnancy.[64] This mistake also negatively affects the child.

Of children born to teenage mothers who never married and who did not graduate from high school, 78% live below the federal poverty level.[62] Additionally, children of teen mothers are more likely to have more health problems, be incarcerated at some time during adolescence, have lower school achievement, dropout of high school, face unemployment as a young adult, and give birth as a teenager themselves.[65]

Anti-abortion legislation is directly responsible for creating a horrible cycle of low-income mothers and children that is endless and supremely difficult to escape. The idea of preventing abortion on the basis of morals leaves entire swaths of the population in worse conditions than they need be. Simply put, the high and mighty approach to pregnancy hurts the poor, and while it carries a good amount of 'Christian values', it holds little in the way of consideration of the well-being of others.

While it's all fine and good to want to 'save a baby', we cannot allow religion to dictate when a medical procedure can or cannot be performed. The only person who should be able to make that decision is the patient themself.

Our representatives don't care what women believe in or want. States that are staunchly anti-abortion believe that women don't know what is best for themselves, especially when given accurate information and easy access to options. States that limit access to clinics and create propaganda that is mandatory to give to women, know that if given the right information and given ample opportunity, many women would choose to have an abortion. State representatives know what choice would be made, so they strip away that choice and, in turn, the freedom that comes with that choice.

Everyone who believes that an individual should have sole power over their own reproductive system, approximately 59% of women and 55% of men,[66] do not matter. Women forced to give birth because of the state they live in, do not matter. Child brides forced to provide a family for an adult twice or more their age, Do. Not. Matter.

Women wanting an abortion are the only people in the United States that are asked to justify their medical choices. They shouldn't have to. Legislation of any kind simply does not belong in a doctor's visit. All medical decisions should be kept between a doctor and their patient. Not a patient and their husband, not a patient and their parents, not a patient and their state representatives - just a patient and their doctor.

It is not a difficult concept. At least, it is not as difficult of a concept as trying to explain why someone should be allowed a voice in a stranger's examination room.

While abortion is technically legal, what we need is a specific law protecting the right to an abortion. We need a law that in clear and direct language states that the government should have no involvement in a woman's choice. It is clear that we cannot depend on the ruling of Roe v Wade to protect women's rights any longer. The regulations and restrictions passed in various states have proven that such general and vague instructions on what a state may, or may not, do to influence the actions of a pregnant woman results in the right to an abortion being denied to many Americans. The system has failed to protect these women and it is time that our legislators fully endorse a straightforward and equitable policy.

Concluding Statement

The world thinks of the United States as a bastion of freedom, but in reality we are spitting on that reputation every day. We are only as free as our legislative branch's morals will allow us. Most of our freedoms are contingent upon the approval of Christianity, despite the fact that 29.4% of Americans are not Christians.[67] We wage war on countries, lambasting them for implementing such things as Sharia law, while we have our very own version brought to the voting floor every day.

I am not against Christianity - you should be able to follow any teachings you believe in. I am not advocating for everyone to go out and get high. I am not advocating for everyone to go prostitute themselves or get an abortion on a whim.

I am advocating freedom - true, personal freedom. I am advocating the idea that your government should not have the power to tell you how to live your life.

To tell someone they may not have a medical procedure performed on themselves, is to tell someone they are not in control of their body. To tell someone they may not make money by selling their body, is to tell someone they are not in control of their body. To tell someone that they may not ingest something, is to tell someone they are not in control of their body.

To tell people that they will be viewed as criminals in the eyes of the law if they do certain things to their own body, is to tell people that **the law** is what controls their bodies.

The idea that our laws are shaped by morals often held by a minority of Americans, and actively work to keep people in prison and in poverty, goes against the very core of democracy and tramples over the tenets of religious freedom that first brought our ancestors to seek a new world.

As Americans, it is our duty to educate ourselves about the restrictions of freedom currently enforced by our government. It is our duty to unequivocally condemn any and all attacks on the personal freedoms due to each individual self. We must educate ourselves and defend our bodies from the government, as it is all too clear that the government seeks to control the American people through propaganda, diversions, delays, and flat-out refusal to carry out the will of constituents. We must demand these rights, rights that should never have been denied at all.

To not defend our own bodies is to not only deny unalienable rights to millions, but to deny these freedoms their sacred place in our hearts and in our country.

Bibliography

1.   https://www.niaaa.nih.gov/alcohol-health/overview-alcohol-consumption/alcohol-facts-and-statistics
2.   https://www.drugabuse.gov/related-topics/trends-statistics/overdose-death-rates
3.   https://www.iii.org/fact-statistic/facts-statistics-alcohol-impaired-driving
4.   Mark Thornton, Alcohol Prohibition Was A Failure (CATO Institute, 1991)
5.   U.S. Bureau of the Census, Historical Statistics of the United States, Colonial Times to 1970 (Washington: Government Printing Office, 1975), part 1, p. 414
6.   Mark H. Moore, Actually, Prohibition Was A Success (New York Times, 1989)
7.   Clark Warburton, The Economic Results of Prohibition (New York: Columbia University Press, 1932), pp. 23- 26, 72.
8.   Ken Burns, Lynn Novick, Prohibition (PBS)
9.   http://www.drugpolicy.org/issues/making-economic-sense
10.   http://www.drugpolicy.org/issues/drug-war-statistics
11.   https://www.prisonpolicy.org/reports/money.html
12.   https://news.gallup.com/poll/221018/record-high-support-legalizing-marijuana.aspx - Justin McCarthy, Record-

High Support For Legalizing Marijuana Use In U.S. (Gallup, 2017)

13. https://www.colorado.gov/pacific/revenue/colorado-marijuana-sales-reports

14. https://www.cpr.org/news/story/where-does-all-the-marijuana-money-go-colorado-s-pot-taxes-explained - Ann Marie Awad, Where Does All The Marijuana Money Go? Colorado Taxes Explained (Colorado Public Radio, 2018)

15. http://www.latimes.com/style/la-marijuana-updates-20170822-california-could-see-a-643-million-1515615929-htmlstory.html - Patrick McGreevy, California Could See A $643 Million Marijuana Tax Haul in First Full Year Of Legalization, Govenor Jerry Brown Says (Los Angeles Times, 2018)

16. https://www.seattletimes.com/seattle-news/politics/state-weighs-using-pot-revenue-to-plug-school-funding-gap/ - David Gutman, Is Marijuana Money The Answer To Fund Washington Schools? (Seattle Times, 2017)

17. https://www.bizjournals.com/boston/news/2018/06/29/mass-recreational-marijuana-sales-could-generate.html - Jessica Bartlet, Mass. Recreational Marijuana Sales Could Generate $219M In Taxes In First Two Years (Boston Business Journal, 2018)

18. http://www.drugpolicy.org/are-more-people-becoming-dependent-marijuana

19.   https://www.drugabuse.gov/publications/drugfacts/m
arijuana

20.   http://www.drugpolicy.org/sites/default/files/heroinfa
cts_03_18_0.pdf

21.   https://www.washingtonpost.com/graphics/2017/heal
th/opioids-scale/?noredirect=on&utm_term=.86fed853a6ed -
Dan Keating and Samuel Granados, See How Deadly Street
Opioids Like 'Elephant Tranquilizer' Have Become
(Washington Post, 2017)

22.   https://www.washingtonpost.com/news/wonk/wp/20
17/08/11/study-one-in-eight-american-adults-are-
alcoholics/?utm_term=.f3e9bef407b4 - Christopher Ingraham,
One In Eight American Adults Is An Alcoholic, Study Says
(Washington Post, 2017)

23.   Journal of Psychoactive Drugs, 44 (2), 125–133, 2012
Copyright © Taylor & Francis Group, LLC ISSN: 0279-1072
print / 2159-9777 online DOI: 10.1080/02791072.2012.684624

24.   http://news.bbc.co.uk/2/hi/uk/8255418.stm - Danny
Shaw, Heroin Supply Clinic 'Cuts Crime' (BBC, 2009)

25.   https://www.theguardian.com/world/2018/jan/14/lega
l-marijuana-medical-use-crime-rate-plummets-us-study -
Jamie Doward, Legal Marijuana Cuts Violence Says US Study,
As Medical Use Laws See Crime Fall (The Guardian, 2018)

26.   https://www.ibtimes.co.uk/sex-law-expert-belinda-
brooks-gordon-why-nordic-model-prostitution-does-not-
work-1434028 - Hannah Osborne, Sex Law Expert Belinda

Brooks-Gordon: Why The Nordic Model Of Prostitution Does Not Work (International Business Times, 2014)

27.   https://www.telegraph.co.uk/men/thinking-man/11169544/Are-we-doing-enough-to-protect-male-sex-workers.html - Gareth May, Are We Doing Enough To Protect Male Sex Workers? (The Telegraph, 2014)

28.   https://tonic.vice.com/en_us/article/evm5vw/nearly-one-in-five-sex-workers-are-men Justin Lehmiller, Nearly One In Five Sex Workers Are Men (Tonic, 2018)

29.   https://www.amnesty.org/download/Documents/POL3 040622016ENGLISH.PDF - Amnesty International, Policy On State Obligations To Respect, Protect, And Fulfill The Human Rights Of Sex Workers, p9 (2016)

30.   https://www.harpersbazaar.com/culture/politics/a200 67359/why-prostitution-should-be-legal/ - Jennifer Wright, Why Prostitution Should Be Legal (Harper's Bazaar, 2018)

31.   https://www.nytimes.com/roomfordebate/2012/04/19/is-legalized-prostitution-safer/nevadas-legal-brothels-make-workers-feel-safer - Barbara G. Brents, Nevada's Legal Brothels Make Workers Feel Safer (New York Times, 2014)

32.   https://amp.businessinsider.com/legal-prostitution-in-nevada-photos-of-brothels-marc-mcandrews - Harrison Jacobs, A Photographer Who Spent 5 Years At Nevada's Brothels Found Legal Prostitution Was Nothing Like What He Thought (Business Insider, 2017)

33.   https://amp.businessinsider.com/why-america-should-legalize-prostitution-2013-11 - Erin Fuchs, 7 Reasons Why America Should Legalize Prostitution (Business Insider, 2013)

34.   http://sexworkersproject.org/downloads/2012/201204 17-public-health-crisis.pdf

35.   https://www.rollingstone.com/politics/politics-news/5-reasons-decriminalization-protects-sex-workers-rights-91292/ - Margaret Huang, 5 Reasons Decriminalization Protects Sex Workers' Rights (Rolling Stone, 2016)

36.   https://thenevadaindependent.com/article/the-indy-explains-how-legal-prostitution-works-in-nevada - Michelle Rindels, The Indy Explains: How Legal Prostitution Works In Nevada (Nevada Independent, 2018)

37.   https://www.amnesty.org/download/Documents/POL3 040622016ENGLISH.PDF - Amnesty International, Policy On State Obligations To Respect, Protect, And Fulfill The Human Rights Of Sex Workers, p10 (2016)

38.   https://www.huffingtonpost.co.uk/alex-bryce/petite-jasmine-sex-workers_b_4439049.html - Alex Feis-Bryce, Why I Will Be Thinking About Petite Jasmine On December 17th, The International Day To End Violence Against Sex Workers (Huffington Post UK, 2014)

39.   https://www.theguardian.com/society/2017/nov/25/po p-up-brothels-britain-sex-industry-suburban - Dulcie Lee,

How 'Pop-Up' Brothels Transformed Britain's Suburban Sex Industry (The Guardian, 2017)

40.	https://www.thenation.com/article/amnesty-international-calls-for-an-end-to-the-nordic-model-of-criminalizing-sex-workers/ - Melissa Gira Grant, Amnesty International Calls For An End To The 'Nordic Model' Of Criminalizing Sex Workers (The Nation, 2016)

41.	http://www.nswp.org/sites/nswp.org/files/Swedish%2 0Law%20to%20Criminalise%20Clients_A%20Failed%20Exper iment%20in%20Social%20Engineering_2012.pdf - Ann Jordan, The Swedish Law to Criminalize Clients: A Failed Experiment in Social Engineering (Program on Human Trafficking and Forced Labor, Center for Human Rights & Humanitarian Law, 2012)

42.	http://files.unaids.org/en/media/unaids/contentassets/ documents/unaidspublication/2009/JC2306_UNAIDS-guidance-note-HIV-sex-work_en.pdf - Joint United nations Programme on HIV/AIDS, p31 (2012)

43.	https://nypost.com/2018/09/28/sex-doll-brothel-blocked-from-opening-in-texas/ - Lia Eustachewich, Sex Doll Brothel Blocked From Opening In Texas (New York Post, 2018)

44.	https://www.usatoday.com/story/news/nation-now/2018/10/03/sex-robot-brothel-blocked-houston-texas/1518298002/ - Joel Shannon, Proposed 'Sex Robot Brothel' Blocked By Houston Government: 'We Are Not Sin City' (USA Today, 2018)

45.   https://amp.usatoday.com/amp/1083444002 - Helena Bachmann, Sex In The City: Zurich's Prostitution 'Sex Boxes' Deemed Success In Switzerland (USA Today, 2018)

46.   https://www.washingtonpost.com/news/wonk/wp/2014/07/17/when-rhode-island-accidentally-legalized-prostitution-rape-and-stis-decreased-sharply/?utm_term=.1ed584eeec4c - Max Ehrenfreund, When Rhode Island Accidentally Legalized Prostitution, Rape Decreased Sharply (Washington Post, 2014)

47.   https://www.businessinsider.com/how-many-abortion-clinics-are-in-america-each-state-2017-2 - Rebecca Harrington and Skye Gould, The Number Of Abortion Clinics In The US Has Plunged In The Last Decade - Here's How Many Are In Each State (Business Insider, 2017)

48.   https://www.nytimes.com/interactive/2018/07/20/us/mississippi-abortion-restrictions.html - Audrey Carlsen, What It Takes To Get An Abortion In The Most Restrictive U.S. State (New York Times, 2018)

49.   https://www.plannedparenthood.org/files/3013/9611/5870/Abortion_Roe_History.pdf - Planned Parenthood Federation Of America p2 (2014)

50.   https://broadly.vice.com/en_us/article/nz88gx/a-state-by-state-list-of-the-lies-abortion-doctors-are-forced-to-tell-women - Callie Beusman, A State By State List Of The Lies Abortion Doctors Are Forced To Tell Women (Broadly, 2016)

51.   Guttmacher Institute, Requirements for Ultrasound, 2018

52.   https://www.apa.org/topics/abortion/index.aspx

53.   https://www.nimh.nih.gov/health/publications/postpar tum-depression-facts/index.shtml

54.   https://www.ncbi.nlm.nih.gov/pubmed/20483973

55.   https://www.pbs.org/newshour/nation/half-u-s-women-say-want-child-survey-reveals - Laura Santhanam, Half Of All U.S. Women Say They Want To Have A Child, Survey Reveals (PBS News Hour, 2016)

56.   https://www.cdc.gov/pregnancy/diabetes.html

57.   https://www.economist.com/graphic-detail/2018/04/23/a-typical-american-birth-costs-as-much-as-delivering-a-royal-baby

58.   https://www.theguardian.com/us-news/2018/jan/16/why-does-it-cost-32093-just-to-give-birth-in-america - Jessica Glenza, Why Does It Cost $32,093 Just To Give Birth In America? (The Guardian, 2018)

59.   https://www.npr.org/sections/health-shots/2015/03/09/391877614/states-fund-pregnancy-centers-that-discourage-abortion

60.   https://www.thenation.com/article/about-half-of-us-states-set-no-minimum-age-for-marriage/ - Michelle Chen, About Half of US States Set No Minimum Age for Marriage (The Nation, 2017)

61.   http://apps.frontline.org/child-marriage-by-the-numbers/ - Anjali Tsui, Dan Nolan, and Chris Amico, Child Marriage In America (PBS, 2017)

62.   https://www.urban.org/urban-wire/preventing-teen-pregnancy-can-help-prevent-poverty

63.   https://www.hhs.gov/ash/oah/adolescent-development/reproductive-health-and-teen-pregnancy/teen-pregnancy-and-childbearing/index.html

64.   https://www.cdc.gov/teenpregnancy/about/social-determinants-disparities-teen-pregnancy.htm

65.   https://www.cdc.gov/teenpregnancy/about/index.htm

66.   http://www.pewforum.org/fact-sheet/public-opinion-on-abortion/

67.   http://www.pewforum.org/religious-landscape-study/

68.   http://ftp.iza.org/dp6226.pdf - Randall Akee, Transnational Trafficking, Law Enforcement and Victim Protection: A Middleman Trafficker's Perspective (IZA, 2010)

69.   https://www.humanrightsfirst.org/resource/human-trafficking-numbers

70.   http://eprints.lse.ac.uk/45198/1/Neumayer_Legalized _Prostitution_Increase_2012.pdf Seo-Young Cho, Does Legalized Prostitution Increase Human Trafficking? (London School of Economics and Political Science, 2012)

71.   https://data.guttmacher.org/states/table?state=AR+ID +NE+OK+UT&topics=57+58+59&dataset=data

Additional sources

72.   Addiction Research and Theory, October 2013; 21(5): 435–442 Copyright 2013 Informa UK Ltd. ISSN: 1606-6359 print/1476-7392 online DOI: 10.3109/16066359.2012.733465

73.   https://www.nytimes.com/roomfordebate/2012/04/19/ is-legalized-prostitution-safer/labor-laws-not-criminal-laws- are-the-solution-to-prostitution - Carol Leigh, Labor Laws, Not Criminal Laws, Are The Solution To Prostitution (New York Times, 2012)

74.   https://www.huffingtonpost.com/cas-mudde/the- paternalistic-fallacy_b_9644972.html - Cas Mudde, The Paternalistic Fallacy Of The "Nordic Model" Of Prostitution (Huffington Post, 2016)

75.   https://www.huffingtonpost.co.uk/ruth- jacobs/prostitution- laws_b_4851224.html?guccounter=1&guce_referrer_us=aHR 0cHM6Ly93d3cuZ29vZ2xlLmNvbS88&guce_referrer_cs=6HuPs uxCGkDL74KdUfVeCg - Ruth Jacobs, The Swedish Model Of Criminalizing The Purchase Of Sex Is Dangerous: The European Parliament Should Have Rejected It (Huffington Post, 2014)

76.   https://nypost.com/2018/10/04/houston-blocks-first-us-based-sex-robot-brothel/ - Reuters, Houston Blocks First US-Based Sex Robot Brothel (New York Post, 2018)

77.   https://www.theguardian.com/us-news/2018/sep/30/houston-robot-brothel-plan-halted - Associated Press in Houston, Houston Officials Halt Plans To Open First US 'Robot Brothel' (The Guardian, 2018)

78.   https://www.theguardian.com/us-news/2018/oct/01/houston-robot-brothel-kinky-s-dolls-sex-trafficking - Tom Dart, 'Keep Robot Brothels Out Of Houston': Sex Doll Company Faces Pushback (The Guardian, 2018)

79.   https://supreme.justia.com/cases/federal/us/410/113/

80.   https://www.guttmacher.org/fact-sheet/state-facts-about-abortion-missouri

81.   https://www.medicalnewstoday.com/articles/237109.php - Christian Nordqvist, What To Know About Postpartum Depression (Medical News Today, 2018)

82.   https://www.nytimes.com/2017/05/26/opinion/sunday/it-was-forced-on-me-child-marriage-in-the-us.html - Nicholas Kristof, 11 Years Old, A Mom, And Pushed To Marry Her Rapist In Florida (New York Times, 2017)

83.   Kamala Kempadoo, Trafficking and Prostitution Reconsidered: New Perspectives on Migration, Sex Work, and Human Rights (2015)